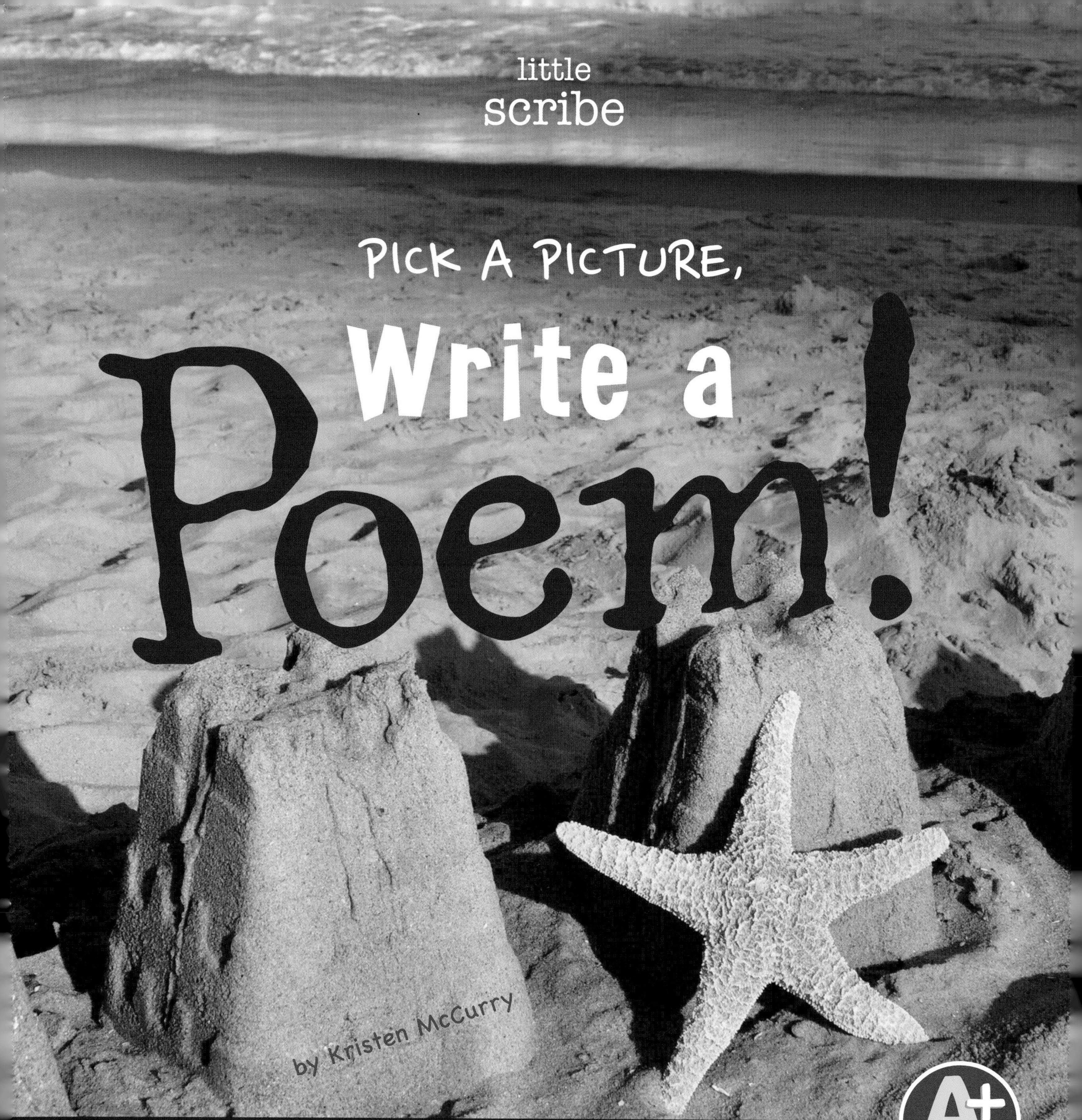

little
scribe

PICK A PICTURE,

Write a Poem!

by Kristen McCurry

A+
books

CAPSTONE PRESS
a capstone imprint

A+ Books are published by Capstone Press,
1710 Roe Crest Drive, North Mankato, Minnesota 56003
www.capstonepub.com

For Annika. —KM

Library of Congress Cataloging-in-Publication Data
McCurry, Kristen.
Pick a picture, write a poem! / by Kristen McCurry.
pages cm. — (A+ Books: Little Scribe)
Includes index.
Audience: Ages 5-8.
Summary: "Introduces poetry writing to children using photographs as idea prompts"— Provided by publisher.
ISBN 978-1-4765-4237-9 (library binding)
ISBN 978-1-4765-5104-3 (paperback)
ISBN 978-1-4765-5949-0 (eBook PDF)
1. Poetry—Authorship—Juvenile literature. 2. Photographs—Juvenile literature. I. Title.
PN1059.A9M35 2014
808.1—dc23   2013032322

Thanks to our adviser for her expertise, research, and advice:
Kelly Boswell, reading consultant and literacy specialist

Editorial Credits
Kristen Mohn, editor; Heidi Thompson, designer; Charmaine Whitman, production specialist

Photo Credits
iStockphotos: DebbiSmirnoff, 24, Vetta Collection/Images_Bazaar, 28; Shutterstock: Blend Images, 8, Carlos Amarillo, 22, Cherry-Merry, 26-27, Daniel Alvarez, cover, 5, Daniel Prudek, 23, emin kuliyev, 12, Everett Collection, 20-21, Henrik Larsson, 14, Ivan Chudakov, 11, Kletr, 6-7, lilyling1982, 18-19, Pete Saloutos, 29, Sebastian Knight, 21 (inset), StacieStauffSmith Photos, 1, Steffen Foerster, 17, Vitaly Titov & Maria Sidelnikova, 30

Note to Parents, Teachers, and Librarians
This Little Scribe book uses full color photographs and a nonfiction format to introduce the concept of writing poems. *Pick a Picture, Write a Poem!* is designed to be read aloud to a pre-reader or to be read independently by an early reader. Photographs help listeners and early readers understand the text and concepts discussed. The book encourages further learning by including the following sections: Table of Contents, Glossary, Read More, Critical Thinking Using the Common Core, and Internet Sites. Early readers may need assistance using these features.

Printed in the United States of America in Stevens Point, Wisconsin.
092013   007773WZS14

Table of Contents

What Is a Poem?

What do you think of when you think of a poem? Do you think of writing that rhymes? Poems can rhyme, but they don't have to. Poems can be many different things. They can be short or long, silly or serious, simple or fancy. They can be about anything at all. Poems are just creative ways to show feelings or ideas. And anyone can write one!

Three little ducks

all in in a line

bobbing for lunch

showing their behinds!

Details Tell More

Some poems tell a little story. Other poems describe something. But all poems should have details. A detail is a small part of something that helps describe it. Details help the reader see and feel what you mean. The hum of your mother's voice or the squeak of your favorite swing are details that make poems stronger.

Red, yellow, orange, and white,

a tiny village shining bright

like a rainbow in between

the light blue sky and dark blue sea,

the high gray hills and tall green trees,

the silver clouds and you and me.

Write with Your Senses

Sight, sound, smell, taste, and touch. Our five senses tell us everything about the world. You can also use them in your poems. Try writing a poem about a certain taste or smell—maybe the smell of your favorite meal cooking, or the taste of salt on your lip on a hot summer day.

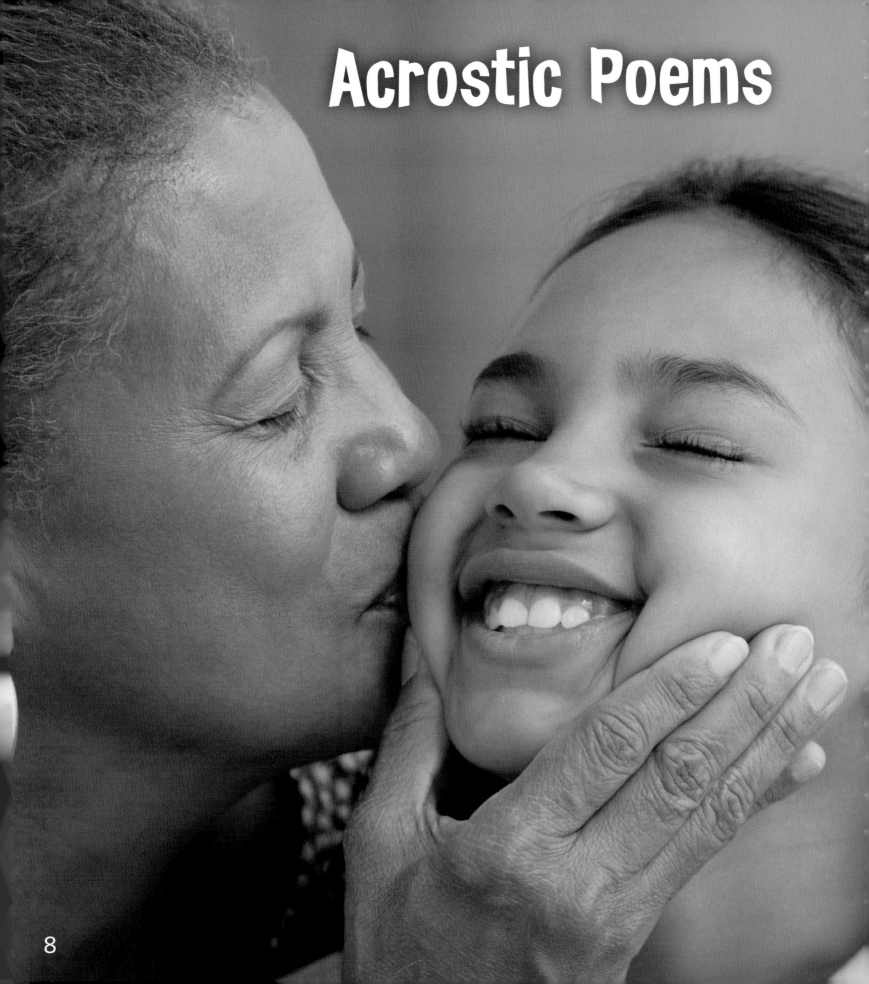

Acrostic Poems

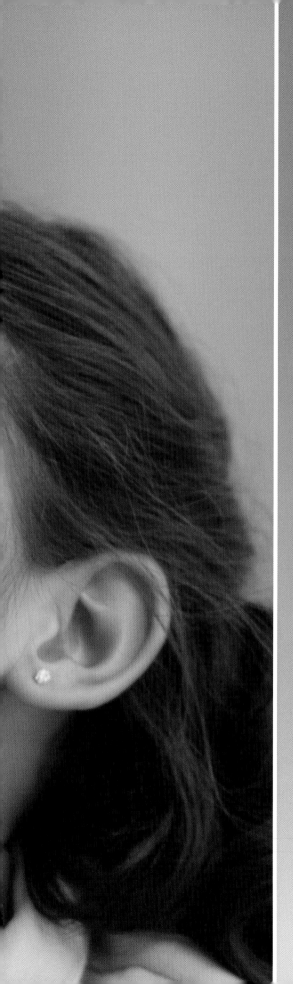

An acrostic is a poem about a topic or a person. The poem uses the letters in the topic word to begin each line. All of the lines tell something about the topic. Here is an acrostic about a grandma.

G ood storyteller

R eally wise

A partment that's cozy

N ever mad

D elicious cookies!

M ine

A lways

Try making an acrostic poem with your name. Each line can tell something about you.

Old Rhyme, New Rhyme

An easy way to come up with an idea for a poem is to borrow an old one. Take a nursery rhyme or a song you know, then change it to make it your own.

> Row, row, row your boat
> gently down the stream.
> Uh-oh, there's a waterfall.
> Now it's time to scream!

Rhyme Patterns

In a rhyming poem, it's often the last word of each line that rhymes. Sometimes the first and second lines rhyme, and the third and fourth lines rhyme. In this poem, the second and fourth lines rhyme ("stream" and "scream"). You can try other rhyming patterns too.

Can you think of another rhyme you can use to make a new poem?

Synonym Poems

A synonym is a word that has a close meaning to another word. You can use synonyms to make up a poem. Pick a word or idea, then think of synonyms for it. See if you can put them together to make a little poem.

This poem plays with synonyms for "fall." The underlined words are synonyms.

I <u>wiped out</u>.

I took a <u>tumble</u>.

I had an <u>accident</u>.

I <u>crashed</u>. I <u>fell</u>.

It didn't go well.

My bike now has a dent.

Make a List

You can make a list of synonyms you might use in your poem. If you're writing a poem about an elephant, you might want to think of synonyms for the word "big":

- large
- huge
- giant

- enormous
- great
- massive

You can also make a list of rhyming words. If a line in your poem ends in the word "big," you can make a list to help find a rhyme:

- dig
- fig
- gig
- jig

- pig
- rig
- twig
- wig

You could make a very silly poem using some of these words!

Haiku

A haiku (hi-KOO) is a type of poem from Japan. It always has three lines. Haiku poems are often about nature or seasons.

How to Write a Haiku

Each line has a certain number of syllables. A syllable is a word or part of a word that makes a single sound.

Line 1: 5 syllables

Line 2: 7 syllables

Line 3: 5 syllables

Here is a haiku about a sneaky spider.
Can you count the 5-7-5 pattern?

Hey you, peek-a-boo!

I see you—do you see me?

Hiding in plain sight.

Try your own haiku!

Free Verse

A poem doesn't have to rhyme or have a certain number of lines. A poem just has to tell about something in a creative way. Free verse is a kind of poetry that doesn't have rules.

Mr. Tree, all twisty and bent,

did you take a wrong turn?

Nature meant you to grow up

but you are growing over!

This poem pretends to talk to the tree. In poetry you can talk to trees—and the trees can talk back! A free verse poem is a wonderful way to show what's in your imagination.

Holiday Poems

Holidays are full of fun, family, good times, and special memories. And those are great topics for poems! Write a free verse poem about your favorite holiday. Be sure to use words in your poem that capture the action, excitement, and feelings of the holiday.

Strong Word Choices

Poems are all about the words. The more interesting words you choose, the better! Below is a list of powerful words you could use in a poem about this photo.

- sizzle
- spark
- flash
- bang

- boom
- burst
- crackle
- pop

Can you think of others?

19

Funny Poems

Some poems can make you smile or even laugh. Looking at silly pictures is a good way to come up with an idea for a funny poem. Your poem might be a riddle. A riddle ends with a question that the reader must answer. Can you think of an answer to this riddle poem?

Noodles, noodles,
oodles of noodles.
Would you care to share?
Meet me in the middle ...
What happens when we get there?

Now try writing a funny poem about this cow.

Clue Poems

In some riddle poems the writer pretends to be something and ends the poem by asking readers to guess what it is.

I buzz.

I bumble.

Flowers are my friends!

I go home to make honey,

then buzz back out again.

What am I?

Try writing a riddle poem about a clock. But remember—don't use the word "clock" in your poem. Your readers have to guess, using the clues you give them.

List Poems

Did you know you can make a poem from a list? Your list can be about anything—your pet, your school, your favorite book. Make your list interesting by including fun details. You can rearrange your list as you go until it sounds just right. Then you've got a poem!

A ball of yarn

A pokey mouse

A bird with lots of feathers

A tasty treat

A pretty collar

A new couch made of leather!

A bell to ring

A string to chase

A sniff of smelly trash!

A sunny spot

A soft bed ...

But please, not a bath!

Soft Rhymes

Rhymes don't have to be perfect. Look at the words "trash" and "bath" in this poem. It's not a perfect rhyme—it's a near rhyme. The words sound kind of alike, but not exactly. "Trash" and "crash" would be what's called a perfect rhyme. You can try different kinds of rhymes and see how they sound to you. In poetry, you don't have to be perfect.

Try writing a poem about a long grocery list. Don't forget to include some funny items.

How-to Poems

A how-to poem is a creative way to teach how something is done. It might be a funny poem about how to peel a banana. Or it might be a serious poem about how to care for someone who's sick.

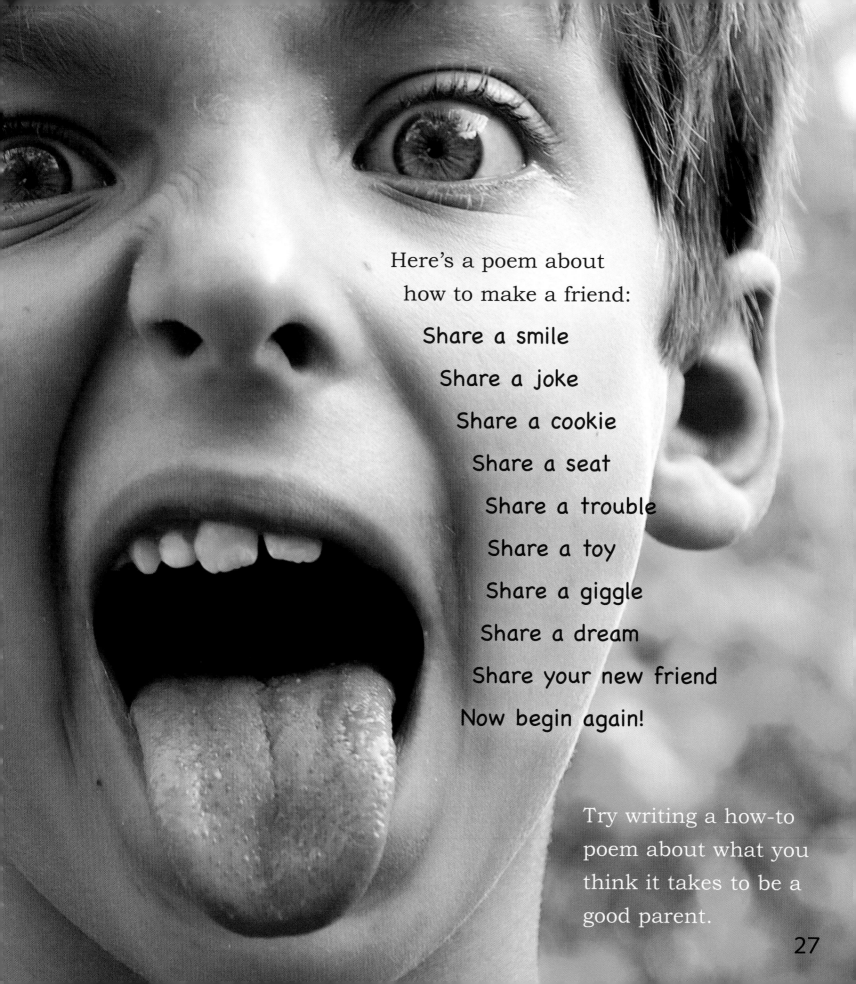

Here's a poem about
how to make a friend:

Share a smile

Share a joke

Share a cookie

Share a seat

Share a trouble

Share a toy

Share a giggle

Share a dream

Share your new friend

Now begin again!

Try writing a how-to
poem about what you
think it takes to be a
good parent.

27

Poems with Feeling

Some of the best poems are ones that show lots of feeling. A poem can be a great way to write about a big feeling, such as pride or love or excitement. Can you feel the writer's excitement in this poem?

My cousins are coming!
My cousins are coming!
I can't wait to see them, I can't!
We'll blow some soap bubbles
and jump in mud puddles
and show wriggly worms to our aunt!

Imagine what it feels like to win a race. Try writing a poem about that feeling.

Look around and you will find ideas for poems everywhere. You could write a poem about your baby brother eating mushy green peas. Or you could write a poem about the silly outfit your neighbor's dog wears!

Keep working on your poems. The more you practice writing poems, the better you will get!

Glossary

acrostic—a poem that uses the first letter of each line to spell out a word; all the lines relate to the topic of the word spelled

describe—to tell about something

detail—pieces of information; small parts of a bigger thing

free verse—a poem that follows no form or subject rules

haiku—a three-line poem that follows a 5-7-5 pattern of syllables

rhyme—word endings that sound the same

riddle—a statement or question that makes you think and that often has a surprising answer

sense—a way of knowing about your surroundings; hearing, smelling, touching, tasting, and sight are the five senses

syllable—a unit of sound in a word

synonym—a word that means the same thing, or almost the same

topic—the subject of a piece of writing

Read More

Fandel, Jennifer. *You Can Write Cool Poems*. You Can Write. Mankato, Minn.: Capstone Press, 2012.

Manushkin, Fran. *It Doesn't Need to Rhyme, Katie: Writing a Poem with Katie Woo*. Katie Woo, Star Writer. North Mankato, Minn.: Picture Window Books, 2014.

Minden, Cecilia, and Kate Roth. *How to Write a Poem*. Language Arts Explorer Junior. Ann Arbor, Mich.: Cherry Lake Pub., 2011.

Critical Thinking Using the Common Core

- Read the poem on page 6. On which sense—sight, sound, smell, taste, or touch—does the poem focus? Explain how the poet uses that sense to paint a picture of the subject. (Key Ideas and Details)

- Study the list of synonyms for the word "big" on page 13. Make a similar list of synonyms for the world "small." (Craft and Structure)

- Look at the photo of the cat on page 24, and read the poem on page 25. Explain how the photo might have inspired the poem. (Integration of Knowledge and Ideas)

Internet Sites

FactHound offers a safe, fun way to find Internet sites related to this book. All of the sites on FactHound have been researched by our staff.

Here's all you do:

Visit *www.facthound.com*

Type in this code: 9781476542379

Super-cool stuff!

Check out projects, games and lots more at
www.capstonekids.com